AL-GHAZZALI
ON THE TREATMENT OF
ANGER, HATRED AND ENVY

Ḥujjat al-Islām Abū Ḥāmid
Muḥammad Ghazzālī Ṭūsī

TRANSLATED FROM THE PERSIAN BY
MUHAMMAD NUR ABDUS SALAM

INTRODUCTION BY
LALEH BAKHTIAR

SERIES EDITOR
SEYYED HOSSEIN NASR

GREAT BOOKS OF THE ISLAMIC WORLD

Library of Congress Cataloging-in-Publication Data

Ḥujjat al-Islām Abū Ḥāmid Muḥammad Ghazzālī Ṭūsī (AH450/CE1059 to AH505/CE1111), commonly known as al-Ghazzali. *Al-Ghazzali On the Treatment of Anger, Hatred and Envy* from the *Alchemy of Happiness (Kimiya al-saadat)*, the Persian translation by al-Ghazzali of the *Ihya ulum al-din (Revival of the Religious Sciences)*

1. Islamic psychology. 2. Sufism. 3. Islamic theology—Early works to 1800. 4. Ghazzali, 1058-1111. I. Title.

ISBN: 1-57644-697-3 pbk

Cover design: Liaquat Ali
Cornerstones are Allah and Muhammad connected by *Bismillāh al-Raḥmān al-Raḥīm* (In the Name of God, the Merciful, the Compassionate).

Logo design by Mani Ardalan Farhadi
The cypress tree bending with the wind, the source for the paisley design, is a symbol of the perfect Muslim, who, as the tree, bends with the wind of God's Will.

Published by
Great Books of the Islamic World, Inc.
Distributed by
KAZI Publications, Inc.
3023 W. Belmont Avenue
Chicago IL 60618
Tel: 773-267-7001; FAX: 773-267-7002
email: info@kazi.org /www.kazi.org

INTRODUCTION

There is nothing more timely today than a translation of the remarkable work on Islam of al-Ghazzali for two reasons. First of all, the results of recent studies of medicine-psychology and religious belief[1] confirm that the religious model works in the healing process so traditional wisdom must be made available in English for all researchers as well as readers to be able to access it and draw upon it for areas of further research. Secondly, at a time when the world is confused by the varying beliefs of Muslims and are interested in studying what the majority of the world's Muslims believe, the works of al-Ghazzali provide the perfect opportunity.

Abu Hamid Muhammad al-Ghazzali was born in the city of Tus, northwestern Iran, in AD 1058.[2] He studied in Tus until he was twenty-seven when he moved to Baghdad. He was appointed as a professor at the Nizamiyyah college there when he was thirty-three. After four years of a strenuous schedule, he underwent a spiritual experience which convinced him that all of the knowledge he had gained was useless in comparison to gnosis or experiential knowledge of the Divine Presence. He realized unless he left his position and was free to search for this knowledge deeper within himself without worldly distractions, he would never attain it. He therefore provided for his family and left for Damascus and other well known cities at that time.

When he was forty-eight he returned to his birthplace where he lived for the next five years until his early death at the age of fifty-three.[3] He left behind over 400 works among them being his famous *Revival of the Religious Sciences (Ihya ulum al-din)* which he wrote in Arabic. Over 2300 pages, it is a compendium of Islamic practices. A few years after he finished the *Revival*, he felt the need to write the same sort of compendium on being a Muslim in Persian. This is the entire work here translated into English for the first time which al-Ghazzali called the *Alchemy of Happiness*. It is a masterful textbook on traditional psychology.[4]

NOTES TO THE INTRODUCTION

1 See works like *Timeless Healing: The Power and Biology of Belief* by Herbert Benson; *Why God Won't Go Away: Brain Science and the Biology of Belief* by Andrew Newberg, Eugene D'Aquili and Vince Rause; and *Handbook of Religion and Health* edited by Harold G. Koniz, Michael McCullough and David B. Larsen.

2 Other well known writers and poets born in Tus include Abu Yazid Bistami, Husayn bin Mansur Hallaj, Abu Said Abi'l-Khayr, Nizam al-Mulk, Firdawsi and Umar Khayyam.

3 See Bibliography below for the numerous books that detail the life of al-Ghazzali. It is interesting to note that al-Ghazzali wrote the *Alchemy of Happiness* when the First Crusade ruled Jerusalem. Saladin arrived on the scene seventy-seven years after al-Ghazzali's death.

4 Traditional psychology was historically called the science of ethics or practical wisdom (*hikmat al-amali*).

SHORT BIBLIOGRAPHY

al-Ghazzali. *Ihya ulum al-din (Revival of the Religious Sciences)*. Translated by al-Hajj Maulana Fazul ul-Karim. Lahore: Islamic Publications Bureau, n.d.

al-Ghazzali, *Incoherence of the Philosophers*. Translated by Michael E. Marmura. A parallel English-Arabic text. Provo, Utah: Brigham University Press, 1952.

al-Ghazzali. *Inner Dimensions of Islamic Worship*. Translated from the *Ihya ulum al-din*. Leicester; Islamic Foundation, 1990.

al-Ghazzali. *Letters of al-Ghazzali*. Translated by Abdul Qayyum. Lahore: Islamic Publications (Pvt), Ltd. , 1994.

al-Ghazzali. *Mishkat al-anwar*. Translated by W. H. T. Gairdner. Lahore: Sh. Muhammad Ashraf, 1991.

al-Ghazzali. *Ninety-nine Beautiful Names of God (al-Maqsad al-asna fi sharh asma Allah al-husna*). Translated by David B. Burrell and Nazih Daher. Cambridge: Islamic Texts Society, 1999.

al-Ghazzali. *On Disciplining the Soul and the Two Desires.* Translated from the *Ihya ulum al-din* (*Kitab riyadat al-nafs. Kitab kasr al-shahwatayn*) by T. J. Winter. Cambridge: Islamic Texts Society, 2001.

Benson, Herbert. *Timeless Healing: The Power and Biology of Belief.* NY: Simon and Schuster, 1996.

Ethical Philosophy of al-Ghazzali. Muhammad Umar ud-Din. Lahore: Sh. Muhammad Ashraf, 1991.

Faith and Practice of al-Ghazzali. W. Montgomery Watt. Edinburgh: Edinburgh University Press, 1952. An abridged translation of *Munqidh min ad-dalal* (Deliverance from Error) and the Beginning of Guidance (*Bidayat al-hidayah*).

Fakhry, Majid. *Al-Ghazzali's Theory of Virtue.* NY: SUNY, 1985.

Koniz, Harold G., Michael McCullough and David B. Larsen. *Handbook of Religion and Health.* NY: Oxford University Press, 2001.

Newberg, Andrew, Eugene D'Aquili and Vince Rause. *Why God Won't Go Away: Brain Science and the Biology of Belief.* NY: Ballantine Books, 2002.

AL-GHAZZALI ON THE TREATMENT OF ANGER, HATRED, AND ENVY

1 ON ANGER

Know that when anger is dominant, it is a reprehensible trait. Its origin is fire and it injures the heart. It is ascribed to Satan, who spoke thus: *"Thou hast created me of fire and him Thou didst create of mud."* (Q. 38:76) The effect of fire is motion and restlessness, while the effect of clay is calm and tranquillity. The relationship of whoever is dominated by anger to Satan is more apparent than his relationship to Adam. It is for this that Ibn Umar, may God be pleased with him, asked the Messenger (☐) "What is that thing which will keep me away from the anger of God Most High?" He said: "That you not grow angry." And he said to the Messenger (☐) "Tell me some act that is simple and hope-giving." (The Messenger) said: "Do not anger!" As often as (Ibn Umar) repeated the question, (the Messenger) gave the same answer. And the Messenger (☐ said: "Anger is as destructive to faith as aloes is to grapes." Jesus (☐ said to a monk: "Do not become angry." (The monk) replied: "I am not capable of that, as I am human." (Jesus) said: "Do not accumulate wealth." (The monk) said: "I am capable of that."

Know that since it is not possible to become completely devoid of the element of anger, suppressing it is a great feat. God Most High said: . . . *And those who control their wrath and are forgiving toward mankind* . . . (Q. 3:134) He praised those persons who suppress their anger; and the Messenger (☐) said: "God Most High controls His punishment for whoever controls his anger. Whenever he begs forgiveness from God Most High, He accepts it. And God Most High covers the shame of whoever restrains his tongue." And he said: "On the Day of Resurrection, God Most High fills the heart of anyone who has the ability to control his anger with contentment when aroused." And he said: "There is a gate to hell which no one enters save the person who gives rein to his anger contrary to the Religious Law." And he said: "Nothing swallowed by His servant is more pleasing to God Most High than anger; none will swallow that save the one whose heart has been filled by God Most High with faith."

Fudayl Iyad, Sufyan Thawri, and company of the saints, may God be pleased with them, are in agreement that there are no acts better than mildness at the moment of anger and forbearance at the time of craving.

Someone was speaking harshly to Umar the son of Abd al-Aziz. (Umar) looked down and said: "Did you wished to enrage me so that Satan may cause me to rise out of pride and sovereignty and give rein to my anger against you this day so that you may give rein to your retaliation tomorrow? That shall never happen!" And he remained silent.

A prophet, peace be upon him, said: "Who will accept this from me and undertake not to become wrathful and become my successor after my death and be my equal in Paradise?" Someone said: "I shall give the undertaking and accept it." (The prophet) repeated what he had said and the man also said that he accepted the terms. He was faithful to his word and became his successor. His was called "Holder of the Pledge" (Dhu al-Kifl) because he had he had given that pledge; that is, he had accepted it.

(1) [THE ROOT OF ANGER WILL NEVER BE UPROOTED]

Know that anger has been created in a person so as to be his weapon in order to stop anything harmful to him; just as appetite was created to be his tool to draw what his beneficial to himself. There is no escape from both of these. However, when they are in excess, they become harmful, resembling a fire which burns in the heart, its smoke rising to the brain, darkening the dwelling of reason and thought so that one does not see the way of right action; just as when smoke enters a cave it makes things so dark that nothing can be seen. This is very reprehensible. Concerning this, it has been said that anger is the ogre of reason.

It may happen that this anger is weak; that too is reprehensible, for the zeal against the forbidden and the enthusiasm for religion against unbelievers arises from (the impulse) of anger. God Most High said to the Messenger (☐): *Strive against the unbelievers and the hypocrites! Be harsh with them!* (Q. 9:73) (God) praised the Companions and said: *(And those with him) are hard against the unbelievers.* (Q. 48:29) All of these are outcome of anger. Therefore, the faculty of anger must not be excessive, nor must it be weak; rather it should be balanced and under the direction of reason and religion.

Some have thought that the objective of asceticism is the rooting out of anger; that is an error, for anger is a weapon and there is no escaping it. The elimination of the impulse of anger is impossible as long as a person is alive, just as the elimination of the impulse of lust is impossible. However, it is lawful to conceal it in certain acts and at certain times so that someone may suppose that there is absolutely no anger. The explanation of this is that the anger arises from someone's attempt to take away something that one needs. However, if there is no need for it, as, for example, a dog which is superfluous, should someone beat or kill it, it is right not to become angered.

But, as for food, residence, clothing, health, and the like, the need for them never ends. Consequently, (if) a person injures these, resulting in a loss of one's well-being, or takes one's food or clothing, anger will necessarily appear. So, the anger of him whose need is greater will be greater and he will be more helpless and impoverished; for freedom lies in need-lessness. However much one's need is greater the nearer one is to slavery. It is possible that a person, through self-discipline, make himself so that his needs are reduced to the absolutely necessary. This results in the elimination from himself of the need for rank, property, and the excesses of the world. Anger will necessarily will follow those needs and depart. For that reason, the person who is not seeking rank is not angered by anyone who has advanced ahead of him or who sits above him in assemblies.

There are great differences among people in this respect, for most anger is connected with the increase of wealth and rank, so that it may happen that a person will boast of something worthless such as chess, backgammon, pigeon-flying, and excessive drinking of wine. If someone says that he does not play chess well, or he does not drink a lot of wine, he will become angry. There is no doubt that whoever is of this kind can be saved by abstention (from those things). However, that which is certain for man is that the impulse of anger does not become eliminated and that itself should not happen, nor is it praiseworthy; but it must not be thus that it deprives a person of his self-control and overpowers his reason and the Law. By self-discipline, one may return anger to this degree. The proof that the impulse of anger does not vanish, nor should it do us, is that the Messenger (⬚) was not lacking in anger He said: "I am a human being. I anger as people anger. I become angry just as a human being becomes angry. Whomever I would curse, or speak harshly to in anger, or strike, O Lord God, turn that into a cause of my mercy upon him."

Abd Allah bin Amr bin al-As, may God be pleased with him, said: "O Messenger of God: 'Should I write down all that you say?' He said: "Write it down, even though I be angry. By that God Who sent me to mankind with the truth, even when I am angry, I utter nothing but the truth." Thus, he did not said: "I have no anger." Instead, he said: "My anger does not take me outside of truth."

One day Ayishah, may God be pleased with her, was angry. The Messenger (⬚ said: "Your devil has come!" She said: "And do you not have a devil?" He replied: "Yes, but God Most High aids me against him so that he is under my control. He does not say anything except the good." He did not say: "I do not have a devil of anger."

(II) [THE TRIUMPH OF GOD'S UNITY CONCEALS ANGER]

Know that even though the root of anger can never be rooted out from the inner being, yet it is right that a person be dominated by God's Unity in some conditions—or most conditions—and consider everything that happens as though it were from God Most High. Then anger is cloaked by God's Unity and nothing of one's own is seen; just as when someone is struck by a stone, in no circumstance does he become angry at the stone, even if the root of anger is entrenched in his inner being, for the stone did not assault him; it was caused by the person who threw the stone. If a ruler signs an order for someone's execution, that person does not become angry at the pen with which the signature was written, because he knows that the pen is employed (by the ruler) and that the pen did not move of itself, even though it moved.

Likewise a person who is dominated by God's Unity necessarily recognizes that all mankind are forced by necessity in that which occurs to them. Indeed, even though movement is controlled by power, yet power is controlled by the will and controlled by desire. The will is not at the disposal of a person; rather, a desire has been imposed upon him, willingly or unwillingly. When the desire has been sent and the power given, the act will necessarily be accomplished. Therefore, it is like the stone which has been thrown at him. The stone causes pain and suffering, but he does not become angry at the stone. Thus, if his sustenance comes from a sheep and the sheep dies, he is troubled but he does not become wrathful. Should someone kill the sheep, if must be the same (to him) if the light of God's Unity dominates.

However, the triumph of God's Unity is not continuous at that limit; rather, it is like a flash of lighting. Human nature becomes apparent in (its) attention to the extant causes. Many people are like that in some circumstances. It is not that the root of anger has been uprooted; when the human perpetrator is not seen, the sorrow of anger does not appear. It is like the stone which hits him. Indeed, it may be that there is no victory of God's Unity involved; rather, one's animal soul is so engaged in a more important work that the anger is obscured and does not become apparent.

A person cursed Salman, may God be pleased with him, (to his face). (Salman) said: "If at the Resurrection the pan of my bad deeds (on the scales of judgment) is heavier, I am worse than what you say. If it is lighter than what you say, what have I to fear?" Someone cursed Rabi Khaytham. (Rabi) said: "Between me and heaven there is an obstruction which I am busy cutting. If I cut it away, what have I to fear from your words? If I do not, what you say is less (bad) than I am." Both of them were so immersed in thinking about the Hereafter that their anger did not show itself.

[A person was cursing Abu Bakr Siddiq, may God be pleased with him. (Abu Bakr) said: "There is much more that is hidden from you." He was so involved with himself that his anger did not appear.] Someone doubted Malik Dinar, may God be pleased with him. (Malik) said: "No one has (truly) known me except you." Someone said something to Shabi, may

God have mercy upon him. (Shaibi) said: "If you speak the truth, may God Most High forgive me. If you lie, may God Most High forgive you."

So, these states show that it is permissible for anger to be suppressed by these states; and it is permissible that one who loves God Most High not become angry with someone unknown. When a cause occurs, the love for God Most High covers his anger. Just as when someone has a beloved who speaks ill of (the lover's) child. The lover knows that he does not want the child to be oppressed and he overlooks it. The triumph of his love is such that he does not take offense at that unkindness and does not become angry.

Therefore, a person must deal with one of these causes so that he kills his anger. If he cannot, he must indeed defeat this impulse so that it not become intractable and act contrary to the Religious Law and reason.

(III) [THE TREATMENT OF ANGER IS OBLIGATORY]

Know that the treatment of anger and disciplining it are a religious obligation, for it carries most people off to hell and from it many are sins are born. Its treatment is of two kinds: (i) The similitude of one (kind) is that of the purgative which tears out its roots and material from within. (ii) The similitude of the other is that of oxymel which soothes and does not carry away matter.

(IV) [THE CAUSES OF ANGER]

As for the purgative, it is that one search out what the internal cause of anger is, tear out its causes by the root; and the causes are five:

(1) The first cause is pride, for the proud person angers at minor lapses of word or treatment against the respect (one feels one is due). This anger must be defeated with humility,

and one must understand that one is of the same genus as other servants (of God); any superiority is of good character. Pride is a bad trait and cannot be expunged save by humility.

(2) The second cause is the vanity in which one is self-absorbed. The remedy is to know oneself. All of the treatments for pride and vanity will be discussed in the appropriate place.

(3) The third cause is jesting which, in most circumstances, leads to anger. One must busy oneself seriously with becoming acquainted with the Hereafter, obtaining a good character, and refraining from frivolity. In the same way, excessive laughter and mockery lead to anger. One must protect oneself from these, for whoever mocks others is mocked himself; therefore, if another mocks him, he has mocked himself.

(4) The fourth cause is casting blame and faultfinding. They also become causes of anger for both sides. Its remedy is that one know that whoever is not without fault should not blame others. No one is without fault.

(5) The fifth cause is the avarice and greed for the increase of property and rank, for with that need becomes great. Whoever is a miser becomes angry when a single grain is taken from him. Whoever is greedy becomes angry if one bite of food is lost to him. All of these are bad traits of character and the roots of anger.

The treatment of these (vices) is both cognitive and practical.

As for the cognitive, it is that one understand its detriment and evil, and the amount of damage it does to him in worldly affairs and in religion, so that it will become repugnant to him in his heart. Then he must occupy himself with the practical treatment. This is so that he will become changed so as to rise up against these traits, for the treatment of all characteristics is opposition (to them), as we have discussed concerning self-discipline.

(A great cause for the provocation of anger and bad traits is association with people who are overcome by their anger. It may be that they call this courage and steadfastness and take pride in it and tell stories: "Such-and-such a great man killed someone for a word and destroyed so-and-so's house and belongings and no one had the courage to say anything against him, because he is a manly man, and men are thus!" Overlooking (slights) is considered self-contempt, dastardly, and unmanly. So they call anger, which is the characteristic of dogs, manliness and bravery; and mildness, which is the characteristic of (God's) messengers, they call dastardly and unmanly!

This is the work of Satan who, with deception and ugly words, keeps (them) away from a good character and invites (them) to a bad character with pleasant words. An intelligent person would know that if the arousal of anger were a part of manliness, then would not women, children, feeble oldsters, and the sick be closer to anger? It is obvious that those people anger more quickly; indeed, there is no manliness greater than that one confront his own anger. This is the attribute of the prophets and saints. The other—it is the attribute of Kurds, Seljuk Turks, and (desert) Arabs, and of people who are closer to predatory animals and beasts. Keep looking to see whether greatness is that which resembles the prophets or that which resembles fools and the negligent!

That which has been said is a purgative, its purpose to void the substance of anger. So, that person who cannot root out that substance must calm it when anger is excited. It may be calmed by an oxymel compounded of the sweetness of knowledge and the bitterness of patience. The treatment for all (personal) traits is a compound of knowledge and action. However, the knowledge is that of the verses (of the Quran) and the Traditions (of the Prophet) which have come down about censuring anger and the spiritual merit for the person who suppresses his anger, reconsiders—as we have described —and says to himself: "God Most High has more power over you than you have over Him, and God's repugnance for you is greater than your repugnance for (the person who incites your anger). If you give rein to your anger (against that person), what surety do you have that at the Resurrection He will not give rein to His anger against you?" As when the Messenger (◻ sent a serving girl on an errand and she returned late. He said: "If it were not for the retaliation at the Resurrection, I would have disciplined you."

Another is that one say to oneself: "Your anger is because the affair proceeded the way God Most High wished, not the way you did; this is contending with the Godhead." If your anger is not stilled with these reasons which are related to the Hereafter, one should marshal worldly motives and say: "If I give rein to my anger, it may happen that he too will be prompted to opposition and retaliate. One should not minimize one's enemy. If, for example, he is a captive who is deficient in service, when he becomes frightened, he may meditate some treachery or conspiracy."

One should also recall one's own ugly image (when angry); how ugly and variable the exterior becomes! It becomes the image of a wolf attacking a person, and its interior becomes all aflame, in the image of a ravenous dog. It usually happens that when one intends to overlook (the offense), Satan says to him: "This will be attributed to your weakness and baseness and will detract from your dignity; you will be held in contempt by the people." One must reply: "No glory comes from that; for a person should take the way of the prophets and seek the pleasure of God Most High. It is better than people despise me in this world today than that I be despised at the Resurrection tomorrow." These and the their like are the theoretical treatment.

As for the practical treatment, it is that one say aloud: I

seek refuge with God from the accursed Satan. The practice (of the Prophet) is that if one is standing one should sit, and if one is sitting, one should lay one's side on the ground. If one does not become calmed from this, one should purify oneself with cold water, for the Messenger (⬚) said: "Anger is of (the nature of) fire; it is extinguished with water." According to one narrative one should prostrate oneself, placing one's face on the earth in order to realize with that (gesture) that one has come from the earth and is a servant (of God) and so that anger will not touch him. One day Umar, may God be pleased, was angered and called for water. He sniffed it into his nostrils and said: "Anger comes from the devil and departs with this." One day Abu Dharr, may God be pleased with him, fought with some one. He said: "O son of the red woman!"—he insulted his mother, saying she was ruddy in color; that is, she was a captive. The Messenger said: "I heard that you insulted someone today through his mother. Know that you are not superior to any black or red person, unless you be more pious than he." Abu Dharr went off to apologize to that person, and that person came and made peace with Abu Dharr.

When Ayishah, may God be pleased with her, would become angry, the Messenger (⬚) would take her by the nose and say: "Dear Ayishah! Say: O God, the Lord of the Prophet Muhammad, forgive me for my sin and expel the anger from my heart and keep me from the turmoil of error." Saying this is also a Practice (of the Prophet).

Know that if a person does some injustice or utters vulgar or terrifying words (to one), it is preferable to remain silent and not respond. However, remaining silent is not a duty, yet not every response is permissible. Indeed, returning curses for curses and maliciously false statements for maliciously false statements is not lawful, for such provocations punishment becomes necessary. But if someone responds in harsh words in which there is no lie, it is lawful; that resembles a kind of legal requital.

Even though the Messenger (☐) has said: "If a person criticizes you in what is true about you, do not criticize him with his faults," this is in the way of a recommendation, and not offering a response is not an obligation when there is no cursing or accusation of adultery. The grounds for this are that the Messenger (☐) said: "Two persons cursing each other, what they have said is upon him who was first until the oppressed one surpasses (him)." He said: "Every two persons who speak unkindly to each other, whatever they say, the one who began is at fault until the injured party exceeds the limits (in his responses). So he should lay off replying before he reaches that point."

Ayishah, may God be pleased with her, used to say: "The wives of the Messenger (☐) gave Fatimah a message: 'Tell the Messenger to be fair among us and Ayishah but you love her more and incline toward her.' The Messenger (☐) had been asleep. He said: 'O Fatimah, do not you not love that which I love?' She said: 'I do.' He said: 'Then love Ayishah because I love her.' Then (Fatimah) went to them and repeated what he had said. They said: 'This does not satisfy us.' Zaynab, may God be pleased with her, was one of the Messenger's wives. She claimed to be my equal in the Messenger (☐)'s love. She was sent by them and said: 'Abu Bakr's daughter does this and that and says unkind things.' I stayed silent in case he might give me permission to reply. When he gave permission, I came in to answer back. I was answering her and speaking unkindly to her until my mouth became dry and she was left helpless. Then the Messenger (☐) said: 'She is the daughter of Abu Bakr.' That is: 'You will not be able to cope with her with words.'"

So, this is the evidence that answering is lawful when it is right and not a lie, as one says: 'Fool! Ignoramus! Be ashamed of yourself and shut up!'' for no person is devoid of foolishness or ignorance. One must train the tongue to be accustomed to using words that are not excessively ugly so that when one is angry, one not resort to vulgarity, as when one says: "Promise-breaker! Turncoat! Knave! Unworthy! Wretch!" and the like. In short, when it comes to answering back, it is difficult to keep within bounds. For this reason is preferred that one not answer back.

Someone was speaking ill of Abu Bakr, may God be pleased with him, in the presence of the Messenger (☐), who remained silent. When Abu Bakr, may God be pleased with him, began to reply, the Messenger (☐) rose. (Abu Bakr) said: "Until now you have been sitting down. Now that I am about to reply you have risen?" He said: "As long as you were silent, an angel was continuously replying on your behalf. Now that you have started to speak, I did not want to sit in the same place with Satan."

And the Messenger (☐) said: "Human beings have been created in different classes. There is one who becomes angry slowly and becomes pleased slowly. There is another who becomes angry quickly and becomes pleased quickly. One is the opposite of the other. The best of you is he who becomes angry slowly and becomes pleased quickly. The worst of you is he who becomes angry quickly and becomes pleased slowly."

2 [ON HATRED]

Know that blessedness follows when someone swallows his anger by means of choice and (the power of) religion; however if he swallows it by reason of weakness necessity, it collects inside him and ferments and turns into hatred. The Messenger (☐) says: "The believer is not hateful." Therefore, hatred is the offspring of anger, and from it eight grandchildren are born, each one of which is a cause of the destruction of religion:

(1) Envy, so that one is saddened by the happiness of that person and made happy by his sorrow.

(2) Malicious joy, that a person rejoice when (his enemy) is afflicted with a calamity, and make that apparent.

(3) That one restrain one's tongue and not reply to the other's greeting of "Peace."

(4) That one look upon him with hatred and scorn.

(5) That one talk about him: backbiting, lying, and insulting; that one lay open that person's private matters and his secrets.

(6) That one mimic him and ridicule him.

(7) That one strike and injure him when the opportunity occurs, or that one persuade someone else to beat him.

(8) That one commit some shortcoming in executing his rights and not honor the connection of kinship, nor repay debts to him, nor turn oppression away from him; and not seek pardon from him.

So, if there is a person whom religion dominates, and who does not commit any sins, there is at least this: that he withholds good deeds from him and does not show friendship to him. He does not aid (the other) in his affairs and does not sit with him for the remembrance of God Most High, nor does he offer (the other person) praise and supplications. All of these things detract from (the aggrieved person's) stature and the harm of this is great. When Mistah, who was a relative of Abu Bakr, spoke about Ayishah, may God be pleased with her, during the incident of the lie. Abu Bakr, who had been paying (Mistah's) stipend, took the money back and swore that he would never give him money again. (At that) this verse was revealed: And let not those who possess bounty and plenty among you, to the place where He said: *Do you not wish that God should forgive you?* (Q. 24:22) (The Messenger) said: "Do not swear that you will not do good to a person who is unkind to you. Do you not desire to like that God Most High will forgive you?" Abu Bakr, may God be pleased with him, said: "By God, I want that!" and he resumed paying the stipend.

Therefore, anyone who harbors a grudge against someone is not free of three concerns: [First], he either struggles against himself in order to do (his enemy) some good deed and increase his consideration—this is the degree of the truly righteous ; or [second], he does not do any good deeds, nor any unbecoming deeds—this is the degree of the abstemious; or [third], he does rude things (to him) and does not do any good things—this is the degree of the vicious and the oppressors. There is no nearness (with God) greater than this: that you do good to the person who does evil to you. If you are not able (to do that), at least forgive him; for the virtue of forgiveness is great.

The Messenger (☐ said: "There are three things that I may swear upon: one is that no property will be lost in (giving) voluntary charity; another is that there is no one who has forgiven a person, upon whom God Most High has not bestowed an increase in honor at the Resurrection; and the third is that no one opens the door of imploring and begging to himself that God Most High does not open the door of poverty (to him). And Ayishah, may God be pleased with her, says: "I never saw the Messenger (☐ retaliate against anyone with respect to himself, but if it detracted from the right of God, his anger had no limit. When choosing between two alternatives, he never chose that which was not easier for the people, unless there was some sin in it." Uqbah bin Amir, may God be pleased with him, used to say: "The Messenger (☐ took my hand and said: 'Should I not inform you what the best behavior of the people of the world and the Hereafter is? That whatever someone takes from you, you give to him; whatever someone deprives you of, you give to him; and that you forgive whoever is unjust to you."

And the Messenger (☐) said that Moses (☐) had said: "O Lord God, who is the more beloved of Thy servants to thee?" He replied: "He who forgives even though he has the power (to retaliate)." And (Moses (☐) said: "Whoever supplicates (God) for misfortune to his oppressor, negates his own rights."

And when the Messenger (☐) conquered Makkah and captured the Quraysh—and they had tormented him very much and they were afraid that they would be executed—he placed his hand on the door of the Kabah and said: "God is One and has no partner. He has fulfilled His promise and given aid to His Own servant and has routed His enemies. What do you see and what do you say?" They said: "What can we say except 'good'? We await your generosity. Today the power is your hands." He said: "I say today that which my brother said. When Joseph (☐) had his brothers in his power, he said: 'No reproach this day shall be upon you. God will forgive you.'" He granted them all security and said: "No one shall bother you."

And the Messenger (☐) said: "When the people stand on the fields of the Resurrection, a herald will cry out: 'Arise! The reward of whoever has forgiven another is with God Most High.' Thousands upon thousands of people shall stand up and enter Paradise without any accounting, for they have forgiven people."

Muawiyah, may God be pleased with him, would say: "When angry be patient so that you may find a great opportunity. When you obtain (the opportunity) and great power, forgive." A person who had committed treason was brought before Hisham. Hisham became angry and said: "Do you quarrel in front of me?" He said: "God Most High has said: On the day when every heart will come disputing for itself. One may dispute before God Most High in stating an excuse; why can that not be done in your presence?" (Hisham) said: "Come and say what you were saying."

Something was stolen from Ibn Masud, may God be

pleased with him. The people were cursing the thief; he said: "O Lord God, if he took if out of some need, let him be blessed by it! If he took for the audaciousness of sinning, let it be his last sin!" Fudayl Iyad, may God be pleased with him, says: "I saw a man whose gold was stolen while he was circumambulating (the Kabah). He was weeping. I said: 'Are you weeping because of the gold?' he replied: 'No, I visualized him standing with me at the Resurrection not having any excuse.' I felt mercy for him." A group of prisoners were brought before Abd al-Malik. One of their chiefs said: "God Most High gave you what you loved most, and that was victory. Now you give what He likes most, and that is forgiveness." And he forgave them all.

Therefore, when anger appears, one must forgive. One most be kind in affairs so that anger itself (has no need to) appear. The Messenger (☐) said: "O Ayishah, whoever has had a portion kindness has found his portion of religion and the world. Whoever has been deprived of kindness has remained deprived of the good of the world and religion." And he said: "God Most High is a friend and He loves kindness. That which is given with kindness is never given with harshness." Ayishah said: "One should observe kindness is all affairs, for nothing which is touched by kindness does not become adorned by it. Kindness should not be cut off in any matter, lest it turn ugly."

3 [ON ENVY]

(I) ENVY AND ITS HARMS

Know that hatred arises from anger and envy arises from hatred. Envy is one of the destroyers. The Messenger (☐) said: "Envy consumes good deeds as fire consumes dry wood." And he (☐) said: "There are three things of which no one is devoid:

suspicion, bad omens, and envy. Let me teach you what their treatment is: When you have a suspicion, do not make yourself an investigator and do not fixate upon it. When you take a bad omen, do not have confidence in it. When envy appears, restrain your tongue and hand from having anything to do with it." And he (◻) said: "That which destroyed many peoples before you has begun to appear among you; that is envy, enmity, and hostility. By the God in Whose command is the heart of Muhammad, you will not enter heaven so long as you do not have faith. And you will not have faith so long as you do not love one another. Let me inform you how this is achieved: Greet one another with 'peace,' openly."

Moses (◻) saw a man under the shade of the Throne. (Moses) yearned for that man's spot and said: "He is one of God's beloved persons." (Moses) asked (God): "Who is he and what is his name?" (God) did not give his name and said: "I shall inform thee of his acts: He never envied another, he never disobeyed his mother and father, and he never made maliciously false statements calculated to damage another's reputation."

Zechariah (◻) said: "God Most High says: 'The envier is the enemy of My bounty, he becomes angry at My decrees and does not like the apportioning that I have made among (My) servants."

The Messenger (◻) said: "Six classes of people go to hell for six sins without any reckoning: oppressive rulers, partisan Arabs, the prideful rich, deceiving merchants, ignorant villagers, and envious scholars."

Anas, may God be pleased with him, says: "One day I was sitting with the Messenger (◻). He said: 'This moment one of the people of heaven will enter.' A man from among the Helpers entered. His shoes were hanging from his left hand and water was dripping from his beard and mustache because he had purified himself. The next day (the Messenger) said the same thing and the man appeared again. This happened three times. Abd Allah bin Amr bin al-As, may God be pleased with him, wanted to know about his actions. He approached him and said: 'I have fought with my mother and father and I would like to stay with you for three nights.' (The man) replied: 'So be it.' (Abd Allah) watched him during those three nights and saw no unusual behavior except that he would wake up and remember God Most High. Then, he said to him: 'I have not fought with my father, but the Messenger (⬚) say such-and such things about you. I wanted to become acquainted with your actions.' He said: 'It is what you have seen.' When I went away, he called to me. He said: 'There is one thing: I have never envied anyone for something he has gotten.' I exclaimed: 'So, your degree is from that!'"

Awn bin Abd Allah, may God be pleased with him, was giving advice to a king. He said: "Keep away from pride for it is the first sin committed against God. It was out of pride that Iblis refused to prostrate himself before Adam. Keep away from greed, for Adam was expelled from heaven because of his greed. Keep away from envy, for the first blood that was shed unjustly was done so out of envy, when the son of Adam slew his brother. And when there is talk of the Companions, or of the attributes of God Most High or stars are discussed, keep silent and hold your tongue."

Bakr bin Abd Allah, may God be pleased with him, says: "There was a man (at the court of) a king. Every day he would stand up and say: 'Do good to the doer of good; the bad deeds of the doer of bad will suffice; leave him to his own deeds.' That king valued him for those words. Someone envied (the adviser) and said to the king that (the adviser) had said that a bad smell came from the king's mouth. The king said: 'What is the proof of this?' He said: 'It is that you summon him to yourself and see that he puts his hand on his nose so as not to smell the odor.' Then (the envier) came and took (the adviser) to his house and gave him food in which there was garlic. Then the king summoned (the adviser). He put his hand over his mouth. (The king) supposed that (the envier) had spoken the truth. It was the custom of the king that no one other himself would write important decrees. He wrote to one of his captives: 'Cut off the head of the deliverer of this letter. Stuff his skin with straw and send it to me.' He wrote it, sealed it and gave it to (the adviser). When he went out, that envier saw him cheerful. He said: 'What is that?' (The other) said: 'The decree of the king.' (The envier) said: 'Let me have it." (The other) said: 'All right.' (The envier) took it from him and delivered it to that official. (The official) said: "In this there is a command that I kill you and fill the skin of your head with stray and send it to the king.' (The envier) cried: 'O God, God! He wrote this about someone else. Refer it to the king.' (The official) said: 'There is no referral in the king's order,' and he slew him. The next day the man stood before the king as usual and said what he usually said. The king was astonished. He said: 'What did you do with that letter?' (The man) replied: 'So-and-so asked me to give it to him.' The king said: 'He told me that you said such-and-such (about me).' (The man) replied: 'I did not say that.' (The king) said: 'Then why did you cover your mouth with your hand?' He said: "That man had given me some food in which there was a lot of garlic.' The king said: 'Go and speak those words as usual: 'Reward the doer of good for his goodness and let the actions of the doer of evil suffice for him.' And it sufficed for that man.'"

Ibn Sirin, may God have mercy upon him, says: "I have not envied anyone for the world, for if one is destined for Paradise, how much is the world itself against the comfort that will come to him? If he is destined for hell, then what benefit is there for him from these comforts when he will go to the fire?"

Someone asked Hasan Basri, may God be pleased with him: "Does the believer envy?" He said: "Have you forgotten the sons of Jacob? A believer envies; if it is a sorrow that he keeps inside his breast and does not let it out by deed, it has no harm." Abu Darda, may God be pleased with him, said: "There is neither happiness nor envy for whoever remembers death often."

(II) THE TRUE NATURE OF ENVY

Know that envy is that you dislike it when someone receives some blessing and you desire that blessing be taken away from them. This is forbidden on the evidence of Traditions and on the evidence that this is repugnance at the decree of God Most High. It is an inner malice; for the desire for the loss of some blessing for another that you will not be yours is nothing other than malice. However, if you desire that you have something like that, but do not wish for its loss to another, and do not dislike (his having) it, then it is called emulation, and also called competition. In religious matters this is praiseworthy and may be an obligation.

God Most High says: *For this let (all) those strive who strive.* (Q. 83:26) And He said: *Race one with another for forgiveness from your Lord.* (Q. 57:21) That is, put yourselves ahead of one another.

The Messenger (☐) said: "There is no envy save for two things: one is (for) the man whom God Most High has granted knowledge and wealth and who continually works with his wealth according to his knowledge. The other is (for) the person to whom knowledge has been given without wealth. He says: 'If I had been given it, I would have done the same.' The reward for both is equal. If the wealth is spent in sin and the other says: 'If it were I, I would have done the same.' The sin for both is the equal."

Consequently, this (type of) competition is also called envy, but there is no displeasure at the blessings of another.

Displeasure is never lawful except for the blessings which the sinner and the oppressor come by which are the instruments of their corruption and tyranny. It is lawful that you desire the loss of (their) blessings; for in reality you have desired the elimination of the tyrant and corruption, not the elimination of the blessings. The sign of this is that when they repent, that displeasure does not linger.

Here there is a point: another person has been given a religious blessing and one desires the same for oneself. When it does not come, it may be that one will disapprove of that difference. So, the elimination of the difference through the loss of that blessing may lighten his heart more than the (other's) retention of the blessing. It is to be feared that one's nature will not necessarily be devoid of this, but when this (feeling) is repugnant, it will be as though if the matter were in his own hands, he would not turn away that blessing from (the other). One will not be held answerable for this much in one's nature.

(III) THE REMEDY FOR ENVY

Know that envy is a great illness of the heart; its remedy is a compound of theory and practice.

(1) As for the cognitive, it is that one know that envy is injurious to oneself—in this world and the next, whilst it is beneficial to the envied person—in this world and the next.

As for that which is detrimental to (the envier) in this world, it is that he is always in (a state of) sorrow, grief, and torment; for every moment (he is concerned) with the blessings that the other receives. He himself is in as much distress as he wishes his enemy to be in. He is in the same situation that he wishes for his own enemy, for there is no sorrow greater than the sorrow of envy. What kind of a fool is it who keeps himself miserable because of his enemy while (the enemy) is not harmed by the envy?

There is a time limit for that (envied) blessing in the decree of God Most High. It is neither before nor after, neither more nor less; for its cause is the eternal decree. Some interpret this as good fortune. Whatever it is called, all agree that there is no alteration of that (divine decree). It is for this that a prophet (☐ when he was afflicted by domineering wife, used to complain to God Most High. A revelation came: "Flee from her until her time expires, for that length of time has been ordained in the eternal decree and cannot be changed." A prophet (☐ was made helpless by calamities; he supplicated and wept much. A revelation came to him: "That day when I decreed the heavens and the earth, this was thy portion. What dost thou say? Should I reapportion it for thee?"

If a person wishes to obliterate (another's) blessing with his envy, the harm comes upon himself, for his own blessings are also obliterated by this envy. Too, envy of the unbelievers obliterates the blessing of one's own faith, as God Most High says: *A party of the People of the Book long to make you go astray*. (Q. 3:69) Therefore envy becomes the coin of the torment of the envier!

However, the damage in the next world is greater, for one's anger is at the decree of God Most High and one's rejection is of his portion, which He has appointed in the perfection of His wisdom. No one can fathom the mystery of that. What betrayal of God's Unity can be greater than this? And then he has rejected the compassion and counsel of the Muslims because he desires misfortune for them. Iblis is his companion in this desire. What evil can be greater than this?

And as for the envied, he has a benefit in this world: it is that what could he wish from this world more than that his envier be always in torment. What torment is greater than envy? No tyrant more resembles the oppressed than does the envier. The envied, if he receives news of your death or that you have been liberated from the torment of that envy, is saddened, for he always wishes to be blessed by being envied while you are in the misery of envy.

As for (the envied one's) religious benefit, it is that he is oppressed by you because of your envy. It may be all that that you act with hostility to him with words. That will be the cause of your good deeds' being transferred to his register and his evil deeds' being placed upon your shoulders. Therefore, (while) you wanted his worldly blessings to depart from him, they did not; and his blessings in the next world have been increased while for you the torment of the world has become immediate and the foundation for the torment of next world has been laid!

So, you supposed him (to be) your own friend and his enemy; but when you looked, [it was the opposite:] he was his friend and your enemy! You keep yourself in misery while gladdening Iblis who is your greatest enemy! When Iblis looked at you and saw that you do not have the blessings of knowledge, piety, rank, and property, he feared that if you were satisfied with that (state of deprivation), the spiritual reward of the Hereafter would come into your possession. He wanted the spiritual reward of the Hereafter also to be lost to you, and it was: for whoever loves the knowledgeable and the religious and is agreeable to their rank and retinue (while he has none) will be among them tomorrow. As the Messenger (☐ says: "Whoever loves someone will be with (that person) tomorrow."

It is said that a man is either a wise person, a student, or their admirer. The envier is deprived of the spiritual reward of all three of these (states). The similitude of the envier is that he is like a person who throws a stone to strike his enemy; it misses him and returns to hit him in the right eye and blind it. His anger increases. Again he throws, harder, and it returns to strike him in the other eye and blind it. He throws (a stone) another time and it returns to strike him on the head. He does this while his enemy is unharmed. His enemies see him and laugh at him. This is the condition of the envier: the object of Satan's derision. All of these are the evils of envy. So, if it leads to raising one's hand and unleashing one's tongue in enmity, slander, lying, and the repudiation of God; its iniquity itself is great. Therefore, whoever realizes that envy will be a fatal poison for himself—if he is intelligent—will let it depart.

(2) As for the practical remedy, is to strive to root out the causes of envy from one's inner being; for the causes of envy are pride, vanity, hostility, the love of rank, and the like, as we have said concerning the essence of anger. These roots must be destroyed through earnest striving; this is the purgative so that the envy itself may definitely not exist. But when it appears, it may be stilled by opposing everything that envy commands. When it commands: "Make some snide remark about him!" one praises him. When it commands: "Slight him!" one gives him aid so that he hears it and his heart is gladdened. When he is pleased, a beam of light (from him) falls upon one's heart in reflection. One's heart is gladdened and the hostility is ended. As God Most High has said: *Repel the evil deed with one which is better, then, lo! he, between whom and thee there was enmity (will become) as though he were a bosom friend.* (Q. 41:34) Here Satan may say to you that if you are humble and you praise him, it will be interpreted as your weakness. You choose: either obey the command of God Most High, or the command of Iblis.

Know that this is a great and potent medicine, but it is bitter. It cannot be endured except through the strength of knowledge by which a person understands that his salvation in religion and the world lies in it, and his perdition in religion and the world lies in envy. No medicine is possible without tolerating bitterness and pain; greed must be cut off with that.

When a disease strikes, the body must be placed in discomfort in the hope of a cure. If not, the disease may lead to destruction, and that is certainly greater than the pain.

(IV) [ENVY MUST BE UPROOTED FROM THE HEART]

Know that if you strive earnestly much, usually you will find a difference between the heart of the person who has troubled you and that of the person who loves you. Comfort and obligation are not equal in your mind; indeed, you will naturally despise the comfort of the enemy. You are not required to change that nature, for it is not in your power; but you are responsible for two things: one is that you necessarily do not disclose this (feeling) by word or deed; and the other is that you dislike this trait in yourself and reject it with your reason, and that you be desirous of the elimination of that trait. When you have done this, you have escaped the sin of envy.

If you do not express it in any manner, but there is a repugnance, because inside you that you continue to find this trait in yourself, some are of the opinion that you are not accountable for this. The correct view is that you are accountable, for envy is forbidden and this is the work of the animal soul or ego, not the work of the body. Whoever desires pain for a Muslim and sorrows at his happiness will certainly be punished, unless he despises this trait. In that case, he will escape the sin. However, a person escapes envy completely when God's Unity conquers him. For him there is neither friend nor enemy; instead, he sees all with the eye of servitude to God Most High; he sees affairs as all from the One. This state is rare; like lightning which flashes and departs. Usually it does not remain constant.